AAT Professional Diploma in Accounting
Level 4
Management Accounting: Dentrol

First edition June 2016
ISBN 9781 4727 4838 6

British Library Cataloguing-in-Publication Data
A catalogue record for this book is available from the British Library

Published by

BPP Learning Media Ltd,
BPP House, Aldine Place,
142-144 Uxbridge Road,
London W12 8AA

www.bpp.com/learningmedia

Printed in the United Kingdom by

Ashford Colour Press Ltd.
Unit 600, Fareham Reach,
Fareham Road, Gosport,
Hampshire PO13 0FW

Your learning materials, published by BPP Learning Media Ltd, are printed on paper obtained from traceable sustainable sources.

Welcome to BPP Learning Media's AAT **Passcards for Management Accounting: Decision and Control**.

- They **save you time**. Important topics are summarised for you.
- They incorporate **diagrams** to kick start your memory.
- They follow the overall **structure** of the BPP Course Book, but BPP Learning Media's AAT **Passcards** are not just a condensed book. Each card has been separately designed for clear presentation. Topics are self contained and can be grasped visually.
- AAT **Passcards** are **just the right size** for pockets and bags.
- AAT **Passcards focus on the assessment** you will be facing.
- AAT **Passcards focus on the essential points** that you need to know in the workplace, or when completing your assessment.

Run through the complete set of **Passcards** as often as you can during your final revision period. The day before the assessment, try to go through the **Passcards** again! You will then be well on your way to completing the assessment successfully.

Good luck!

		Page

The BPP **Question Bank** contains activities and assessments that provide invaluable practice in the skills you need to complete this assessment successfully.

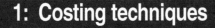

1: Costing techniques

Topic List

Overview of a costing system

Classification of costs by behaviour

High-low method

Under- and over-absorption of overheads

Methods of costing

Costs can be classified in a variety of different ways. Particularly in this chapter we will be looking at the classification of costs according to their behaviour when activity levels change.

Direct cost

A cost that can be **traced in full** to the product, service or department that is being costed.

Direct costs include

- Direct materials
- Direct labour
- Direct expenses
- Total direct costs = prime cost

+

↓

= TOTAL PRODUCT COST

Indirect cost (overhead)

A cost that is incurred whilst making a product but which **cannot be traced directly** to the product, service or department.

Indirect costs include

- Indirect materials
- Indirect labour
- Indirect expenses

Classified as:

- Production overhead
- Administration overhead
- Selling and distribution overhead

Cost centre

A collecting place for costs before they are analysed further.

Once costs have been traced to cost centres they can be further analysed in order to establish a cost per cost unit.

Cost unit

A unit of product or service to which costs can be related.

Example

- Department
- Machine
- Project

Example

- Single product
- Service
- Job
- Contract

Profit centre Area of business which incurs costs and revenues.

Investment centre Area of business which incurs costs and revenues and accounts for its own capital investment.

Costs are influenced by many factors. The most important factor is the level of activity or volume of output.

Level of activity may refer to

- Value of items sold/made
- Number of items sold/made
- Number of hours worked
- Number of invoices issued
- Number of units of electricity consumed

Basic principles of cost behaviour

As the level of activity rises, costs will usually rise. It will generally cost more to produce 200 units of output than it will to produce 100 units of output.

In general, level of activity = volume of output.

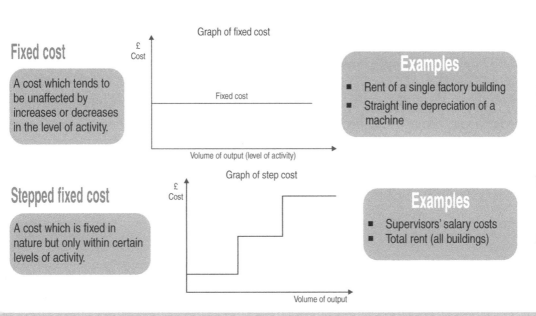

Fixed cost

A cost which tends to be unaffected by increases or decreases in the level of activity.

Graph of fixed cost

£ Cost

Fixed cost

Volume of output (level of activity)

Examples

- Rent of a single factory building
- Straight line depreciation of a machine

Stepped fixed cost

A cost which is fixed in nature but only within certain levels of activity.

Graph of step cost

£ Cost

Volume of output

Examples

- Supervisors' salary costs
- Total rent (all buildings)

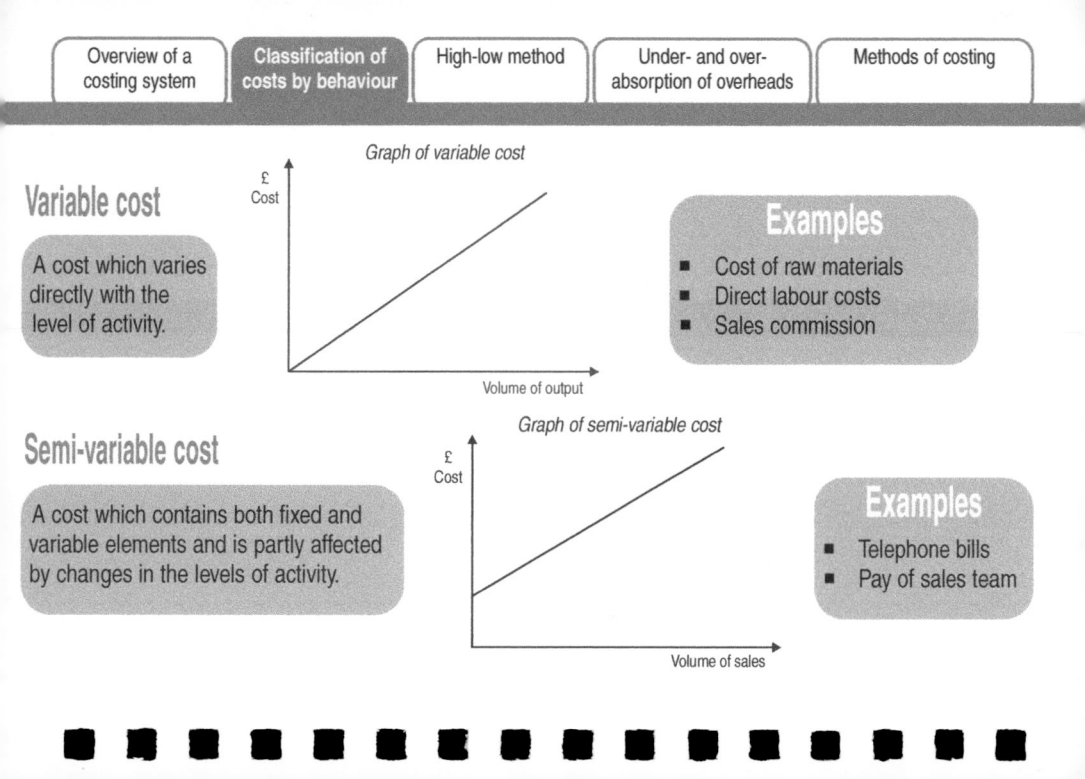

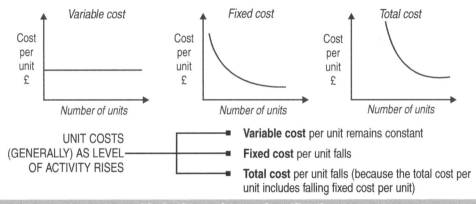

UNIT COSTS (GENERALLY) AS LEVEL OF ACTIVITY RISES

- **Variable cost** per unit remains constant
- **Fixed cost** per unit falls
- **Total cost** per unit falls (because the total cost per unit includes falling fixed cost per unit)

Limitations of cost classification

- Assumes linear relationship.
- Unit variable costs may fall as volumes increase due to economies of scale/discounts or increase eg due to overtime premiums.
- The relevant activity level that causes costs to vary may not always be units of output, eg telephone call costs may vary with number of calls made.

It is generally assumed that costs are one of the following ——— Variable / Fixed ⟹ So semi-variable costs need to be divided into their fixed and variable elements.

The fixed and variable elements of semi-variable costs can be determined by the **high-low** technique.

High-low technique

Step 1. Review past records of costs ——— Select period with **highest** activity level
——— Select period with **lowest** activity level

Step 2. Determine ———
- Total cost at high activity level (TCH)
- Total cost at low activity level (TCL)
- Total units at high activity level (TUH)
- Total units at low activity level (TUL)

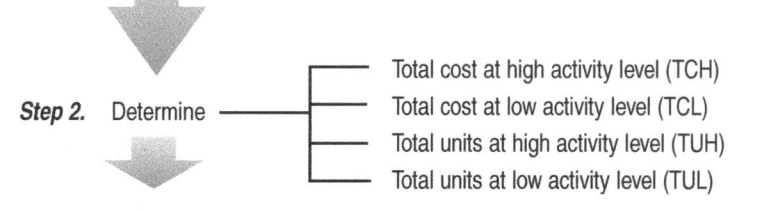

Step 3. Calculate variable cost per unit $= \dfrac{\text{TCH} - \text{TCL}}{\text{TUH} - \text{TUL}}$

Step 4. Determine fixed costs by substituting variable cost per unit at high or low activity level

Example

Highest activity level	= 10,000 units at a cost of £4,000
Lowest activity level	= 2,000 units at a cost of £1,600
Variable cost per unit	$= \dfrac{£(4,000 - 1,600)}{10,000 - 2,000} = \dfrac{£2,400}{8,000} = £0.30$
Fixed cost	$= £4,000 - £(10,000 \times 0.3) = £1,000$

Example

Fixed element of cost steps up by £30,000 when 32,000 or more units are produced.

Highest activity level = 34,000 units at a cost of £208,000
Lowest activity level = 28,000 units at a cost of £160,000

$$\text{Variable cost per unit} = \frac{£208,000 - £30,000 - £160,000}{34,000 - 28,000} = \frac{£18,000}{6,000} = £3$$

Fixed cost at 28,000 units = £160,000 − (28,000 × £3) = £76,000
Fixed cost at 34,000 units = £208,000 − (34,000 × £3) = £106,000

This discrepancy is an adjustment in the income statement at the end of the period.

Over-/under-absorbed overheads

These arise because the OAR is predetermined from budget estimates. When actual overheads incurred and overheads absorbed (using predetermined OARs) are compared, there will be an over- or under-absorption of overheads.

Reasons

(1) Actual OH different from estimated OH

(2) Actual activity level different from estimated activity level

(3) 1 and 2 above (together)

OH = Overheads
OAR = Overhead absorption rate

> Actual overhead − Absorbed overhead =
>
> NEGATIVE ⟶ OVER-ABSORBED
>
> Credit to income statement

> Actual overhead − Absorbed overhead =
>
> POSITIVE ⟶ UNDER-ABSORBED
>
> Debit to income statement

Note: The calculation of absorbed overhead depends on whether the predetermined OAR is on a unit or an hourly basis:

- Actual units produced × standard absorption rate per unit, or
- Actual hours × standard absorption rate per hour

A unit basis for absorption is used in standard costing. An absorption rate based on hours of activity is used in other absorption costing systems.

The objective of absorption costing is to include in the total cost of a product or service an appropriate share of the organisation's production overheads. An 'appropriate share' means an amount that reflects the amount of time and effort that has gone into producing the unit of product or service.

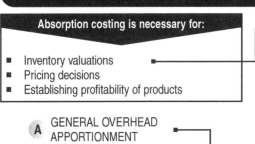

Absorption costing is necessary for:

- Inventory valuations
- Pricing decisions
- Establishing profitability of products

Full absorption means that non-production overheads (selling and distribution, administration and finance expenses) are also absorbed into unit costs. These should **not** normally be included in inventory valuations, which just includes production overheads.

A GENERAL OVERHEAD APPORTIONMENT

B SERVICE COST CENTRE COST APPORTIONMENT

Three stages of absorption costing

(1) Allocation of expenses (costs incurred directly by a cost centre)
(2) Overhead apportionment (costs jointly incurred by a number of cost centres)
(3) Absorption into cost units

Calculating an overhead absorption rate

1 Allocate any specific costs direct to cost centres

eg packing labour to packing department, maintenance labour to maintenance department

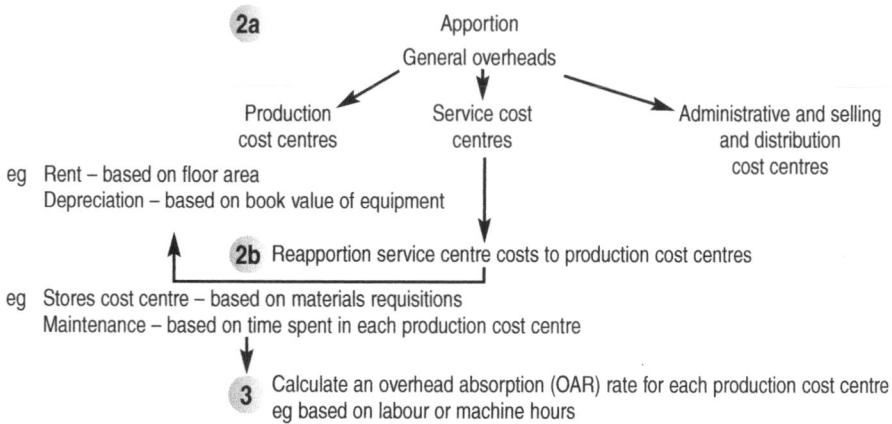

2a Apportion

General overheads

Production cost centres Service cost centres Administrative and selling and distribution cost centres

eg Rent – based on floor area
Depreciation – based on book value of equipment

2b Reapportion service centre costs to production cost centres

eg Stores cost centre – based on materials requisitions
Maintenance – based on time spent in each production cost centre

3 Calculate an overhead absorption (OAR) rate for each production cost centre
eg based on labour or machine hours

Marginal cost

The cost of one unit of product/service which would be avoided if that unit were not produced/provided = variable cost.

Contribution

Sales revenue less variable (marginal) cost of sales. It is short for 'contribution towards covering fixed costs or overheads and making a profit'.

Marginal costing

- Only variable costs charged as cost of sales
- Closing inventory is valued at marginal production cost
- Fixed costs or overheads are treated as period costs
- Period costs are charged in full to income statement
- If sales increase by one item, profit will increase by the contribution of one item
- Contribution per unit is constant at all levels of output and sales

Reporting profit

Absorption costing

Sales		X
Opening inventory	X	
Full production cost of units produced	X	
	X	
Less: Closing inventory	(X)	
Full production cost of sale		(X)
Gross profit		X
Other costs:		
Administration overheads	(X)	
Sales and distribution overheads	(X)	
		(X)
Profit		X

Inventory is valued at full production cost

Marginal costing

Sales		X
Opening inventory	X	
Variable production cost of units produced	X	
	X	
Less: Closing inventory	(X)	
Variable production cost of sale	X	
Other variable overhead costs	X	
		(X)
Contribution		X
Fixed costs		
Production fixed cost	(X)	
Administration fixed costs	(X)	
Sales and distribution fixed costs	(X)	
		(X)
Profit		X

Inventory is valued at variable production cost

The difference in reported profits between marginal costing and absorption costing is calculated as the difference between the fixed production overhead included in the opening and closing inventory valuations using absorption costing.

MARGINAL COSTING ⟶ Closing inventory is valued at marginal production cost

ABSORPTION COSTING ⟶ Closing inventory is valued at full production cost

RECONCILIATION

	£
Marginal costing profit	X
Adjust for fixed overheads included in inventory valuation:	
+ increase / – decrease	X/(X)
Absorption costing profit	X

Inventory levels

Increase in a period

- Absorption costing reports higher profit:
  - More fixed overheads included in closing inventory than in opening
  - So cost of sales of period decreased
  - Hence, profit higher

Decrease in a period

- Absorption costing reports lower profit:
  - Lower fixed overheads included in closing inventory than in opening inventory
  - So cost of sales of period increased
  - Hence, profit lower

1: Costing techniques

Advantages of absorption costing

- Fixed overheads have to be incurred to produce output so fair to share between units produced
- Consistent with the closing inventory value that is required by accounting standards (IAS 2)
- In the long term selling price needs to cover fixed costs to be profitable

Advantages of marginal costing

- Fixed costs are the same regardless of output so sensible to charge them as a period cost
- Does not require arbitrary apportionment of fixed costs
- Avoids under- or over-absorption of fixed overheads
- It focuses on variable costs and contribution which can be more useful for decision making

2: Statistical techniques

Topic List

Time series analysis

Index numbers

Linear regression

In this chapter we will look at some basic statistical methods that you may need to use for this unit.

Time series A series of income or expenses figures recorded for a number of time periods.

Time series analysis A method of calculating the trend from a time series.

Finding the trend (T) using moving averages

Of an odd number of periods

Year	Sales	Moving total of 3 yrs' sales	Moving av. of 3 yrs' sales (÷3) TREND
20X5	390		
20X6	380	1,230*	410
20X7	460	1,290**	430
20X8	450		

* (390 + 380 + 460)
** (380 + 460 + 450)

Of an even number of periods (centred moving average)

Year	Sales	Moving total of 4 yrs' sales	Moving average of 4 yrs' sales	Mid-point of 2 moving averages TREND
20X4	600			
20X5	840			
		2,580*	645.0	
20X6	420			650.00
		2,620**	655.0	
20X7	720			
20X8	640			

*(600 + 840 + 420 + 720) **(840 + 420 + 720 + 640)

Seasonal variation The regular short-term pattern of increases or decreases in figures that repeats due to the nature of the business.

Finding the seasonal variations (S)

Calculate the seasonal variations

- **Additive model** ($Y = T + S$)
  S = actual − trend ($S = Y - T$)

Wk 1	Y Actual	T Trend	S Seasonal variation
Mon	80	92.70	−12.70
Tues	104	93.12	+10.88 etc

Additive model

Actual figure (Y) = Trend (T) + Seasonal variation (S)

Deseasonalised or seasonally-adjusted value = trend (T) = Y – S

Forecast value (Y) = (forecast (T)) + S

Examples

(1) If T = £560,000 and S = –£45,000, forecast = £515,000

(2) Suppose Y for weeks 1 to 4 is 120, 90, 110, 150 and S for weeks 1 to 4 is 20, –20, –10, 20 (with a four-week cycle)

■ Calculate T (deseasonalised or seasonally-adjusted data) for weeks 1 to 4
   Wk 1: 120 – 20 = 100
   Wk 2: 90 – (–20) = 110
   Wk 3: 110 – (–10) = 120
   Wk 4: 150 – 20 = 130

■ Determine increase/decrease in T (increasing by 10 units per week)

■ Forecast T for weeks 5 and 6 (130 + 10 = 140 units, 140 + 10 = 150 units)

■ Adjust T by appropriate seasonal variations to get forecast Y
   (week 5, Y = 140 + 20; week 6, Y = 150 – 20)

Accuracy of forecasts

Examples

- **Aim** – use past data on previous activity/costs/sales to estimate/forecast future.

- Conclusions only valid if sample of historical data is representative. Adjustments for seasonal variations and changes in price levels (indexing) may help achieve this.

- **Interpolation** – estimation of a future figure within the range of data previously observed.

- **Extrapolation** – estimation of a future figure outside the range of data previously observed.

Interpolation is more accurate than extrapolation.

Topic link: forecasting and standards

A forecast value could be compared with a standard currently being used to assess the appropriateness of that standard.

Price index

Measures the change in the money value of a group of items over a period of time.

Eg **Retail Prices Index** which measures changes in the costs of items of expenditure of the average household.

The RPI can be used to restate figures from a time series in terms of current prices eg

$$\text{Current value of sales in year Y} = \text{Actual sales in year Y} \times \frac{\text{Current RPI}}{\text{RPI for year Y}}$$

Index points

Also used to measure the difference in the index value in one year with the value in another year, eg the RPI rose 34 points between 20X0 and 20X3 (100 to 134).

Base period

The base period is also known as the **base year** or **base date** and is usually the starting point of a series.

Base period index = 100 — Should be a 'representative' time

$$\text{Index} = \frac{\text{Current period figure}}{\text{Base period figure}} \times 100$$

Forecasting sales

1. Apply a regression line (trend line) $y = a + bx$, where y = sales and x = period of time.

2. Years (days/months) become the x variable by numbering them from 1 upwards.

3. A forecast (y) for a particular time period (x) is determined by substitution of the value for x into the trend line equation.

Example: sales

Regression line = £400,000 + £300x

Forecast trend for quarter 9 (x = 9) = £400,000 + £(300 × 9) = £402,700

If the seasonal variation in quarter 9 is 40,270, forecast sales are £402,700 + £40,270 = £442,970.

Forecasting costs

A value for x (activity level) can be substituted into the equation and a value for y (total cost at that activity level) forecast.

Example: costs

Regression analysis produces $y = 17 + 3.6x$ (where x is in '000 units and y is in £'000). Fixed costs are therefore £17,000 and variable cost per unit is £3,600.

Predicted cost (y) if activity level (x) is 13,000 units = 17 + (3.6 × 13) = 63.8 = £63,800.

Finding a and b

a and b calculated if two sets of activity/costs are given: same as high-low calculation.

Example

Total production costs are £15,000 for 1,000 units and £25,000 for 2,000 units.

$$y = a + bx$$

$$£15,000 = a + 1,000b$$

$$£25,000 = a + 2,000b$$

subtract £10,000 = 1,000b

$$b = 10,000/1,000 = £10$$

Substitute this in equation

$$£15,000 = a + (1,000 × £10)$$

$$a = £5,000$$

so Total production cost of 1,400 units

$$= £5,000 + (1,400 × £10)$$

$$= £19,000$$

3: Standard costing

Topic List

Standards

Standard costing forms the basis of variance analysis, which is covered in chapters 4 to 6.

It is important that you are able to accurately calculate standard costs.

Standard cost cards

STANDARD COST CARD
Product no 12345

	Cost	Requirement	£	£
Direct materials				
A	£2.00 per kg	6 kgs	12.00	
B	£3.00 per kg	2 kgs	6.00	
				18.00
Direct labour				
Grade I	£6.00 per hour	3 hrs	18.00	
Grade II	£8.10 per hour	5 hrs	40.50	
				58.50
Prime cost				76.50
Variable production overheads	£1.00 per hour	8 hrs	8.00	
Fixed production overheads	£3.00 per hour	8 hrs	24.00	
Standard full cost of production				108.50

What is a standard?

Monetary/rate element × resource element ⟶ Standards for each cost element ⟶ Standard cost of a product

■ ■ ■ ■ ■ ■ ■ ■ ■ ■ ■ ■ ■ ■ ■ ■ ■ ■

Remember the importance of standards in control systems

Types of performance standard

Ideal
- Perfect operating conditions
- Unfavourable motivational impact

Target
- Allowances made for inefficiencies and wastage
- Incentive to work harder (realistic but challenging)

Normal
- Based on current working conditions
- Can lead to stagnation in performance

Basic
- Unaltered over a long period of time
- Unfavourable impact on performance

Possible format of standard costing tasks:

Part 1 You need to be able to use task data provided (presented as either budget or standard cost information) to calculate actual/budget information or standards for use in parts 2 and 3. This allows you to demonstrate that you understand the accounting data provided and that you can see the links between data.

Part 2 This part of the task requires you to calculate variances. A statement reconciling the actual cost of production to the standard cost of actual production is then generally asked for.

Part 3 You are provided with additional data and have to carry out more detailed analysis, often providing your results in a report or memo.

Example to be used in chapter 4 and chapter 6

Presentation approach 1: standard cost data

Standard cost of product A	£
Materials (5 kgs × £10 per kg)	50
Labour (4 hrs × £7 per hour)	28
Variable o/hds (4 hrs × £1 per hour)	4
Fixed o/hds (4 hrs × £6 per hour)	24
	106
Budgeted output	1,200 units

Presentation approach 2: budget data

Product A: budgeted production	£'000
Materials (6,000 kgs)	60.0
Labour (4,800 hrs)	33.6
Variable o/hds (4,800 hrs)	4.8
Fixed o/hds (4,800 hrs)	28.8
	127.2
Budgeted output	1,200 units

Actual results	
Production	1,000 units
Materials	4,850 kgs, £46,075
Labour	4,200 hrs, £29,610
Variable o/hds	£3,800
Fixed o/hds	£25,000
Standard cost of units produced	£106,000

You are likely to be given actual data and **either** standard cost or budget data.

Deriving standard and actual data

- Actual cost per kg of material
  = total actual cost ÷ actual kgs used = £46,075 ÷ 4,850 kgs = £9.50 per kg

- If given data in presentation approach 1, budgeted cost of material
  = standard cost per A × budgeted production = £50 × 1,200 = £60,000

- If given data in presentation approach 2, standard rate per labour hour
  = total budgeted cost ÷ total budgeted hours = £33,600 ÷ 4,800 hrs = £7 per hour

- Standard usage of material for actual output (the amount of material that should have been used for actual output)
  = standard input of material per A × actual output = 5 kgs × 1,000 units = 5,000 kgs

- Standard cost of actual production (used in reconciliation statements)
  = standard cost per unit × actual production level = £106 × 1,000 units = £106,000

If a task mentions the standard or actual **absorption** cost of actual production, this means the total standard or actual cost of actual production *including* fixed overheads (not just standard or actual fixed overheads).

Notes

4: Variance analysis

Topic List

Material variances

Labour variances

Variable overhead variances

Fixed overhead variances

This is an extremely important chapter as the topics covered are likely to come up in every assessment.

You have to be able to calculate all the variances covered here and draw up reconciliation statements.

Material price variance

The difference between what the material purchased should have cost and what it did cost.

Material usage variance

The difference between the material that should have been used and the material that was used, valued at the standard price per unit of material.

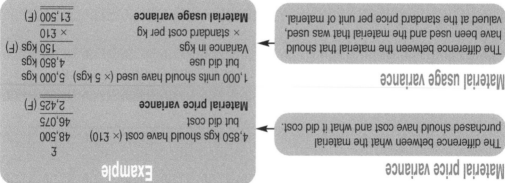

Example

Material price variance

	£
4,850 kgs should have cost (× £10)	48,500
but did cost	46,075
	2,425 (F)

Material usage variance

1,000 units should have used (× 5 kgs)	5,000 kgs
but did use	4,850 kgs
Variance in kgs	150 kgs (F)
× standard cost per kg	× £10
	£1,500 (F)

Don't assume that material variances will be based on kilograms or litres. You may be required to calculate a usage variance for a restaurant or hotel or the product in which the product is a customer or guest and the material is a meal.

If a business purchases more or less material than it uses in production, inventory will arise. Remember the material price variance is based on the quantity of material **purchased** whereas the usage variance is based on the quantity used in production.

Labour rate variance

The difference between what the labour used should have cost and what it did cost.

Labour efficiency variance

The difference between the hours that should have been worked and the hours that were worked, valued at the standard rate per hour.

Example

	£
4,200 hrs should have cost (× £7)	29,400
but did cost	29,610
Labour rate variance	210 (A)

1,000 units should have used (× 4 hrs)	4,000 hrs
but did use	4,200 hrs
Variance in hours	200 hrs (A)
× standard rate per hour	× £7
Labour efficiency variance	£1,400 (A)

Variable overhead expenditure variance

The difference between what variable overheads should have cost and what they did cost for the hours worked.

Variable overhead efficiency variance

The amount of variable overhead spending incurred extra or saved as a result of inefficiency or efficiency in working. Equals the labour efficiency variance in hours, but valued at the variable overhead rate per hour.

Example

	£
4,200 hrs should have cost (× £1)	4,200
but did cost	3,800
Vble o/hd expenditure variance	400 (F)

Efficiency variance in hours: same as for labour	200 hrs (A)
× Standard vble rate per hour	× £1
Vble o/hd efficiency variance	£200 (A)

The total fixed overhead variance is the difference between the overhead incurred and the overhead absorbed into the cost of production (= under- or over-absorbed overhead). There are two reasons why under- or over-absorption occurs.

Budgeted expenditure ≠ actual expenditure

Budgeted output volume ≠ actual output volume

Expenditure variance
Fixed overhead not absorbed into the cost of production but charged to the statement of profit or loss (income statement) because of a difference between budgeted and actual expenditure.

Volume variance
Fixed overhead not absorbed into the cost of production but charged to the statement of profit or loss (income statement) because of a difference between budgeted and actual production volumes (in units).

There are two reasons for a difference between budgeted and actual production volumes (➜ volume variance):

Reason 1

Actual hours worked ≠ budgeted hours
➜ **capacity variance**

Reason 2

Due to efficiency or inefficiency, output in standard hours was more or less than expected ➜ **efficiency variance**

In a standard marginal costing system there is no volume variance, only an expenditure variance.

Total variance = difference between fixed overhead incurred and fixed overhead absorbed
= under- or over-absorbed fixed overhead

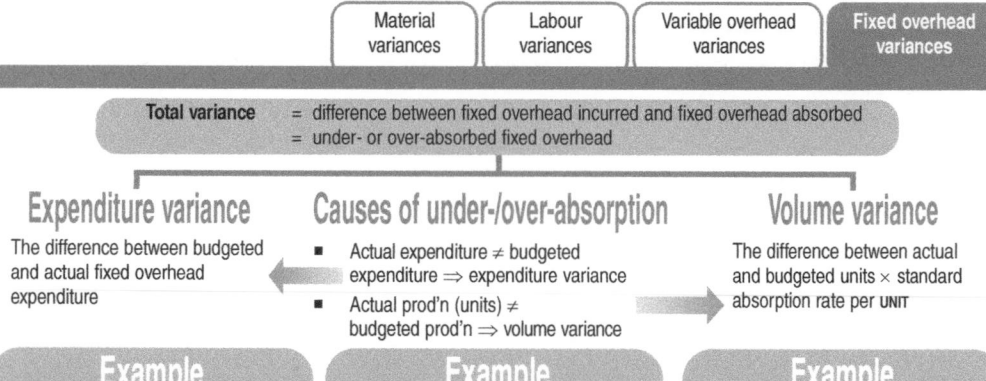

Expenditure variance

The difference between budgeted and actual fixed overhead expenditure

Causes of under-/over-absorption

- Actual expenditure ≠ budgeted expenditure ⇒ expenditure variance
- Actual prod'n (units) ≠ budgeted prod'n ⇒ volume variance

Volume variance

The difference between actual and budgeted units × standard absorption rate per **UNIT**

Example

	£
Budgeted o/hd	
(1,200 × £24)	28,800
Actual overhead	25,000
Expenditure variance	3,800 (F)

Example

	£
Overhead incurred	25,000
Overhead absorbed	
(1,000 × £24)	24,000
Under-absorbed	
overhead/total variance	1,000 (A)*

*(A) because the amount of overhead absorbed by the units is less than the overhead which was actually incurred

Example

	£
Actual prod'n at std rate	
(1,000 × £24)	24,000
Budgeted prod'n at std rate	
(1,200 × £24)	28,800
Volume variance	4,800 (A)*

*(A) because actual output less than budgeted output

Volume variance

Efficiency variance

Shows how much of the volume variance is due to efficiency of labour/plant.

The difference between the number of hours that production should have taken and the number of hours worked × standard absorption rate per HOUR.

Example

Labour efficiency variance in hrs	200 hrs (A)
× standard rate per hr	× £6
Efficiency variance	£1,200 (A)

Cannot be calculated if activity cannot be expressed in terms of hours

This is usually the ← labour efficiency variance in hours

Note the variance is (A) when actual hours are less than → budgeted hours (as less overhead is absorbed).

Capacity variance

Shows how much of the volume variance is due to hours worked being more or less than budgeted (due to strikes, machine breakdowns etc).

The difference between budgeted hours of work and actual hours worked × standard absorption rate per HOUR.

Example

Budgeted hours (1,200 × 4)	4,800 hrs
Actual hours	4,200 hrs
Variance in hrs	600 hrs (A)
× std rate per hr	× £6
Capacity variance	£3,600 (A)

4: Variance analysis

Apportionment of fixed overheads

Budgeted fixed overheads might be apportioned to an organisation's cost centres or to its products/services. The apportionment **takes place before any variances are calculated** and determines the level of budgeted fixed overheads to be used in variance calculations.

Different absorption bases

Units of output of a particular product and labour hours might not always be the basis for volume and capacity/efficiency variances. The volume variance could be based on aircraft flights, the efficiency/capacity variances on machine hours, say.

Subdividing the volume variance

- The efficiency variance in units shows how the efficiency with which resources (labour, machines and so on) were used has affected the volume of output.
- The capacity variance in units shows how the amount of resources used (compared with budget) has affected the volume of output.

In order for the fixed overhead variances to provide meaningful management information, the resource **by which output is measured** (such as labour hours or machine hours) **must be appropriate to the task** in question. It is also important that there is a **link between the output** and the **resource**, that the resource is used to create the output.

5: Operating statements

Topic List

Reconciliation statements

As part of the control process, managers frequently use operating statements to show the link between budgeted and actual performance.

You have to be able to draw up reconciliation statements.

Using absorption costing

	(F)	(A)	£
Std absorption cost of actual prod'n			X
Variances	(F)	(A)	
	£	£	
Material price etc		X	
Fixed overhead expenditure	X		
Fixed overhead capacity	X		
Fixed overhead efficiency		X	
	X̄	X̄	X
Actual absorption cost of prod'n			X̲

Using marginal costing

	(F)	(A)	£
Standard variable cost of actual production units			X
Budgeted fixed costs			X
Variable cost variances	(F)	(A)	
	£	£	
Material price	X		
Material usage, etc		X	
Fixed overhead expenditure		X	
Total cost variances	X̄	X̄	X (A)
		or	(X) F
Actual cost of production			X̲

Advantages of these formats

- Compares like with like (what costs should have been for actual volume of output and what costs were)
- Highlights areas giving rise to differences between planned and actual cost
- Separation of variances into components shows what part of total material variance (for example) is the responsibility of the purchasing manager (price) and what part is the responsibility of the production manager (usage)
- Allows management by exception (ie focussing on items that need attention and ignoring others)

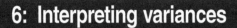

6: Interpreting variances

The contents of this chapter provide the material and techniques required to carry out more detailed analysis of variances.

Variance	Possible causes of FAVOURABLE variance	Management action
Material price	Unforeseen discounts received	Change standard if discounts to continue
	Greater care in purchasing	Ensure improved level of care becomes the norm
	Change in material standard	Change data held on management info system
Material usage	Material used of higher quality than standard	Continue to use higher-quality material if no cost implications
	More effective use made of material	Ensure more effective use becomes the norm
	Errors made in allocating material to jobs	Amend error and improve measurement/recording systems
Labour rate	Use of workers at a rate of pay lower than standard	Change standard if reduction in rate of pay permanent

Variance	Possible causes of FAVOURABLE variance	Management action
Labour efficiency	Output produced more quickly because of worker motivation	Investigate reasons for improved motivation and ensure motivation continues
	Output produced more quickly because of better quality equipment/materials	If use of better equipment/materials to be permanent, change standard
	Errors in allocating time to jobs	Amend error and improve measurement/recording systems
Overhead expenditure	Savings in costs incurred	Promote continued importance of cost control
	More economical use of services	Ensure economical use continues
Overhead efficiency	Resource (labour, machines) more productive than planned	See labour efficiency
Overhead capacity	Resource (labour, machines) used more than planned (eg due to increased demand)	Ensure increase in hours not due to labour inefficiency

Variance	Possible causes of ADVERSE variance	Management action
Material price	Price increase	Change standard/source cheaper supplier
	Careless purchasing	Ensure purchasing staff improve purchasing decisions
	Inflation and seasonal variations in price	Outside buying management's control (amend standard?)
	Rush orders	Investigation into why rush order necessary (and agree only meet rush orders if extra costs covered by higher revenue)
Material usage	Defective material	Change supplier
	Excessive waste	Assess whether workers require more supervision
	Theft	Ensure stores are secure/issues made only if appropriate documentation produced
	Stricter quality control	Change standard if stricter level more appropriate
Labour rate	Wage rate increase	Change standard if increase in rate of pay permanent
	Use of workers at higher grade than standard	Change standard if grade change permanent

Variance	Possible causes of ADVERSE variance	Management action
Labour efficiency	Lost time in excess of standard allowed Output lower than standard because of lack of training/sub-standard material	Improve work flow/reliability of machines etc if lost time is idle time Ensure staff trained to appropriate level/change supplier
Overhead expenditure	Increase in cost or change in type of services	Change standard if increase/change is permanent
Overhead efficiency	Resource less productive than planned	See labour efficiency
Overhead capacity	Resource used less than planned (fall in demand, strike)	Determine reason

Do not learn these causes and actions by rote. You must be able to apply them to the scenario of the task.

Responsibility accounting

The managers responsible for various elements of the business are held accountable for the variances within their control.

In general, when deciding whether or not to investigate a particular variance, bear in mind four points:

- Materiality or significance
- Controllability
- Variance trend
- Interdependence

The cause of one (adverse) variance may be wholly or partially explained by the cause of another (favourable) variance.

- Material price and usage variances
- Labour rate and material usage variances
- Material price and labour efficiency variances
- Labour rate and efficiency variances

Why might variances occur?

- Actual outcome measurement errors
- Out of date standards
- Inefficient or efficient operations
- Random or chance fluctuations (remember that standards are averages)

Further analysis

- Revise standards (index)
- Planning variances: identify variances due to specific fault in the standard (non-controllable) and report controllable variance separately

Here are some examples based on the data on Page 30.

Example

If an index of labour rates stood at 115 when the standard rate of £7 was set and it now stands at 118.45, the percentage increase in labour rates has been $((118.45 - 115)/115) \times 100\% = 3\%$.

	£	£
Actual hours worked at original standard rate $(4,200 \times £7)$	29,400	
Actual hours worked at revised standard rate $(4,200 \times £7 \times 1.03)$	30,282	
Non-controllable variance		882 (A)
Adj price for actual quantity	30,282	
Actual cost	29,610	
Controllable variance due to other reasons		672 (F)
Total labour rate variance		210 (A)

If the standard had been set at the more realistic rate of £7.21 ($£7 \times 1.03$), the variance would have been £672 (F), not £210 (A).

7: Performance indicators

Topic List

Performance indicators

Productivity

Profitability

Working capital

Gearing

Interpretation of ratios

Balanced scorecard

Tasks frequently require you to establish and discuss the types of indicator covered in this chapter.

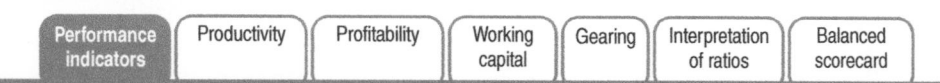

| Performance indicators | Productivity | Profitability | Working capital | Gearing | Interpretation of ratios | Balanced scorecard |

Uses and examples of performance indicators

- Identify problems (direct labour efficiency variance)
- Control costs (distribution as % of revenue)
- Identify how well resources are being managed (idle labour hours)
- Highlight how well the organisation is being managed (profit as % of revenue)
- Planning production and finished inventory levels (number of returns)

Benchmarks against which performance indicators can be compared

- Standards, budgets, targets
- Trends over time
- Results of other parts of the organisation
- Results of other organisations/industry best practice

Data for performance indicators

- Quantitative
- Qualitative

Subjective ———————— Judgemental

The performance measurement process must compare 'like with like'.

Measures of performance using the standard hour

Capacity ratio

$$C = \frac{A}{B}$$

Similar to the fixed o/hd capacity variance and compares actual hours worked with budgeted hours and measures the extent to which planned available resources have been used

(Actual hours worked/budgeted hours) × 100%

Efficiency ratio

$$E = \frac{S}{A}$$

Similar to the fixed o/hd efficiency variance and measures the efficiency of the labour force by comparing standard hours worked and actual hours worked

(Standard hours produced/actual hours worked) × 100%

Activity (production volume) ratio

$$A = \frac{S}{B}$$

Does not compare actual.

Similar to the fixed o/hd volume variance and compares standard hours worked and budgeted hours

(Standard hours produced/budgeted hours) × 100%

$$\text{Capacity ratio} \times \text{Efficiency ratio} = \text{Activity ratio}$$

Value added

Represents the value of output created within the organisation

Value added = sales value – cost of purchased materials and bought-in services

Note: do not deduct cost of employees.

Value added per employee = value added/number of employees

Gross profit margin
(Gross profit/revenue) × 100%

Comment

- Measure of the profitability of sales
- Increased by raising prices and/or negotiating lower prices with suppliers
- Focuses on trading and manufacturing activities
- Limitations: affected by the inventory valuation method used and fails to take account of differences in organisations' cost structures

Operating profit margin or operating profit %
(Operating profit/revenue) × 100%

Comment

- Key measure of efficiency for profit-making organisations
- Measure of the **efficiency** with which revenue (**input**) has been used to generate profit (**value of output**)
- Increased by improving gross profit margin, reducing overheads or increasing sales volumes
- Concerned with profit over which operational management can exercise day to day control (amount left after all direct costs and overheads have been deducted from sales revenue)
- May be an interdependency with the asset turnover ratio
- Limitations: affected by different inventory valuation and depreciation policies and fails to show differences in cost structures

Note: Net profit margin can be calculated based on (Profit after interest and tax/revenue) × 100%

$$ROCE = \frac{\text{Operating profit}}{\text{Total Assets} - \text{Current Liabilities}} \times 100\%$$

(our recommended method)

- Major measure of efficiency of profit-making organisations
- Measures **efficiency** with which capital employed (**input**) used to generate profit (**value of output**)
- If ROCE is 30%, 30p of profit is generated for every £1 of capital invested
- Increased by improving profit margins and/or increasing asset turnover

Note: Return on net assets (RONA) is calculated as $\dfrac{\text{Profit after tax}}{\text{Total Assets} - \text{Current Liabilities}} \times 100\%$

Asset turnover

Calculated as (sales/capital employed) where capital employed = (non-current assets + net current assets) or (long-term liabilities + capital).

This is a key measure of **productivity** for many asset based organisations, measuring how intensively capital employed has been used to generate sales.

'New' non-current assets and/or a large non-current asset base can raise productivity but will reduce ROCE and asset turnover.

Asset turnover is expressed as 'n times' so that assets generate n times their value in annual revenue.

Link between ROCE, profit margin and asset turnover

ROCE = Operating profit margin × asset turnover

ROCE can be increased by improving the profit margin and/or increasing asset turnover

Liquidity ratios

Current ratio

= current assets/current liabilities should usually be >1 otherwise the business may not be able to pay its debts on time.

Quick (or **acid test**) **ratio**

= (current assets − inventory)/current liabilities

Used for businesses where inventory turnover is slow.

- Trend is important
- Ratio can be too large as well as too small

Ratios for control of receivables, payables and inventory

Average age of receivables or **receivables' days** or **receivables' collection period** is calculated as:
(trade receivables/revenue) × 365 days (or × 12 mths)

- This gives a rough measure of the average length of time it takes for a company's receivables to pay what they owe.

- Trend is important.

- Supermarkets' ratio should be low, exporting companies' probably high.

- Limitation: statement of financial position figure used for receivables might not be representative of the whole period.

Average age of payables or **payables' days** or **payables' payment period** is calculated as:
(payables/cost of sales) × 365 days (or × 12 mths)

Purchases can be used as an alternative to cost of sales if the amount of purchases is given in the exam.

- This gives a rough measure of the average length of time it takes for a company to pay what it owes.

- It helps to assess a company's liquidity. (An increase can be a sign of a lack of long-term finance or poor management of current assets, resulting in use of extended credit from suppliers, increased bank overdraft etc.)

- Limitation: statement of financial position figure used for payables might not be representative of the whole period.

The **inventory holding period** indicates the average number of days for which inventory is held and is calculated as (inventory/cost of sales) × 365 days (or × 12 mths).

An increasing ratio indicates a slowdown in trading or a build up of inventory.

Points to note

- These ratios can provide an insight into working capital control (minimising funds tied up in net current assets while ensuring sufficient inventory, cash and credit facilities for trading).
- These ratios help identify how long it takes to convert purchase of inventory into cash from sales.
- The lower the age, the better the control.
- If the current ratio is too low there may be insufficient inventory and current assets to sustain trade, but taking too much credit may jeopardise relationships with suppliers.
- If the current ratio is too high, the organisation must control receivables, reduce inventory levels and use credit facilities more efficiently.
- Limitations: working capital figure may not be representative and the ratio includes a subjective valuation of inventories.

Gearing ratios

Interest cover = Profit before interest/interest

Indication of how much of annual operating profit is taken up by interest payments

Gearing ratio = Total debt/equity × 100%

OR

$$= \frac{\text{Total debt}}{\text{Total debt} + \text{equity}} \times 100\%$$

You might be asked to calculate one or more ratios which are relevant to the organisation described in the task data. For example, you may have to calculate the percentage room occupancy for a task concerned with the performance of a hotel, or the average age of rent arrears in months for a student housing society (which is simply the average age of receivables). You will be provided with definitions of non-standard ratios.

Comparisons

The performance indicators need to be compared:

- Over time
- Within the organisation
- With target or budgeted figures
- With a similar organisation
- To industry averages

Look at the movements in each ratio, explain why it might have changed and consider how the ratios piece together.

Limitations of ratios

Take care when using ratios to draw conclusions because you need to compare like with like.

Possible issues include:

- Different accounting policies
- Inflation
- Year end figures not representative
- Influenced by significant accounting adjustments
- Age of non-current assets may make comparisons between companies difficult
- Behavioural issues may cause lack of goal congruence if ratios used to assess performance

Perspective	Detail	Examples of performance measures
Financial	Concerned with satisfying shareholders	<ul><li>ROCE</li><li>Gross and operting profit margin</li></ul>
Customer	Measures how customers view the organisation and how they measure customer satisfaction	<ul><li>Delivery speed, measured by time between order and delivery</li><li>Customer loyalty, measured by repeat business ((revenue from regular customers/total revenue) × 100%)</li></ul>
Internal*	Measures the quality of the organisation's outputs in terms of technical excellence and consumer needs	<ul><li>Total quality measurement (reworked faulty production as % of total production)</li><li>Training costs as a % of production costs</li><li>Resource utilisation measures (eg proportion of available hotel rooms occupied)</li></ul>
Innovation and learning**	Emphasises the need for continual improvement of existing products and the ability to develop new products to meet customers' changing needs	<ul><li>Revenue from new products as % of total revenue</li><li>R+D costs as % of total costs/turnover</li></ul>

* Sometimes known as **internal business** perspective
** Sometimes known as **learning and growth** perspective

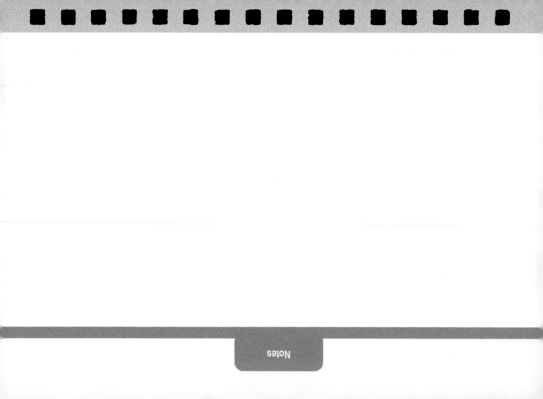

Notes

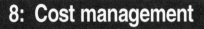

8: Cost management

Topic List

Target costing

Life cycle costing

The contents of this chapter are likely to be tested by a task asking you to describe how the organisation described in task data can use the approaches covered here.

Traditional approach to product costing

1 Develop a product

2 Determine the expected standard production cost

3 Set a selling price (probably based on cost)

4 Resulting profit

Costs are controlled through variance analysis at monthly intervals.

Target costing approach

1 Decide the selling price needed to make the product competitive

2 Decide the required profit margin

3 Set a target for the cost of a product or service which represents the maximum the organisation can incur and sell the product at its target price and still make the desired profit

Determining target cost

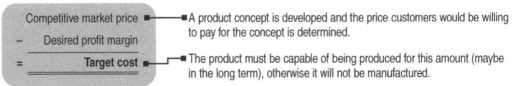

Competitive market price ──■ A product concept is developed and the price customers would be willing to pay for the concept is determined.

− Desired profit margin

= **Target cost** ──■ The product must be capable of being produced for this amount (maybe in the long term), otherwise it will not be manufactured.

During the product's life the target cost will be continuously reviewed and reduced so that the price can fall. Continuous cost reduction techniques must therefore be used.

Example:

Market price	£500
Desired margin (15%)	(£75)
= Target cost	£425

Target cost

If the anticipated product cost (based on the design specifications) is above the target cost, the product must be modified so that it is cheaper to produce.

The total target cost can be split into broad cost categories such as development, marketing, manufacturing and so on. A team of designers, engineers, marketing and production staff, as well as the management accountant, should then endeavour to produce a product with planned development, marketing, manufacturing (and so on) costs below the target costs.

If any of the target costs cannot be achieved given the product design, other individual targets must be reduced, the product redesigned yet again or scrapped.

Options available to reduce cost

- Develop the product in an atmosphere of continuous improvement.
- Apply **value engineering/value analysis techniques**.
- Collaborate closely with suppliers.
- Change production methods.
- Improve technologies/processes.
- Cut out non-value added activities.

Value analysis

This involves assessing the value of every aspect of a product (or service) in order to devise ways of achieving its purpose as economically as possible while maintaining the required standard of quality and reliability.

Value engineering = value analysis at the product design stage

Conventional cost reduction techniques v **Value analysis**

Try to achieve the lowest production cost for a specific product design

Tries to find the least cost method of making a product that achieves its desired function

↓

Aims to get rid of all unnecessary costs = costs that do not add value

↓

Value is only added while a product is actually being processed

Typical considerations

- Can a cheaper (but as good or better) substitute material be found?
- Can unnecessary weight or embellishments be removed without reducing the product's attractiveness or desirability?
- Is it possible to use standardised or fewer components?

→ A value-adding activity cannot be eliminated without the customer perceiving a deterioration in the performance, function or other quality of a product.

Product Life Cycle (PLC)

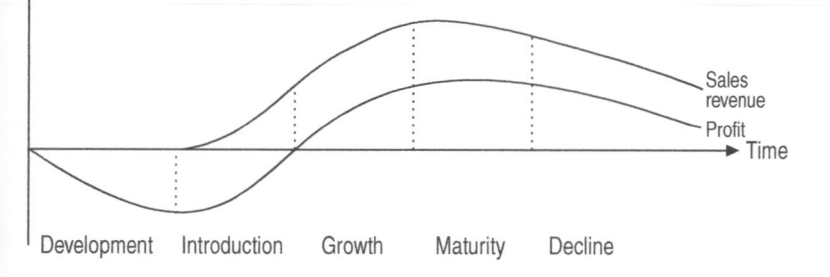

- Most products have a limited life cycle and show different sales/profitability patterns at the 5 different stages.
- Length of life cycle varies depending on the nature of the product and the market.

Life cycle costing

The costs incurred over a product's life cycle can be illustrated by
the generic curves on the diagram below.

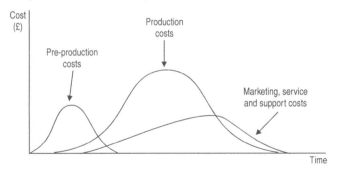

Traditional costing

- Records and analyses costs once production has begun
- Based on series of 12 month accounting periods

Life cycle costing

- Accumulates all costs over the whole life cycle to ensure these are covered by revenue from the product
- May use DCF to account for time value of money

Notes

Topic List

Activity based costing

ABC is an extension of absorption costing specifically considering what causes each type of overhead category to occur.

Outline of an ABC system

1 Identify an organisation's major activities

2 Identify **cost drivers** ■————

3 Collect the costs associated with each activity into **cost pools**

4 Charge support overheads to products on the basis of their usage of the activity (measured by the number of the activity's cost driver they generate)

Cost drivers

Any factor which causes a change in the cost of an activity

Examples

The cost driver for a cost that varies with production volume (such as power costs) should be volume related (eg labour hours or machine hours).

The cost driver for a cost that is related to the transactions undertaken by a support department should be related to that transaction. For example, the cost driver for the cost of setting up production runs is the number of production runs.

Example

Cost of goods inwards department totalled £10,000. Cost driver for goods inwards activity is number of deliveries. During 20X0 there were 1,000 deliveries. 200 of these deliveries related to product X. 2,000 units of product X were produced.

Cost per unit of cost driver = £10,000/1,000 = £10
Cost of activity attributable to product X = £10 × 200 = £2,000
Cost of activity per unit of product X = £2,000/2,000 = £1

9: Activity based costing

10: Decision making techniques

Topic List

CVP analysis

Limiting factor analysis

Make or buy decisions & closures

Discounted cash flow

In this chapter we will look at a variety of ways in which costing information can be used for decision making purposes.

Decision making

- In the short term fixed costs do not change, so decisions should be based on marginal costs
- Profit is maximised by maximising contribution

Contribution per unit

unit selling price – unit variable costs

Profit

(sales volume × contribution per unit) – fixed costs

Breakeven point is the activity level at which there is neither profit nor loss.

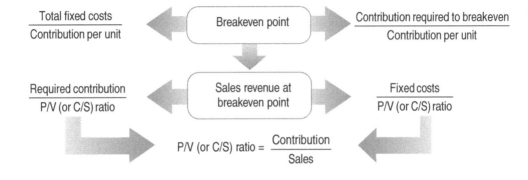

The margin of safety is the difference in units between the budgeted sales volume and the breakeven sales volume and it is expressed as a percentage of the budgeted or actual sales volume.

Example

Selling price = £15 per unit
Variable cost = £12 per unit
Fixed costs = £5,400 per annum
Budgeted sales pa = 3,000 units

- Breakeven point (units) $= \dfrac{£5,400}{£15 - £12} = 1,800$ units

- P/V (or C/S) ratio $= 3/15 \times 100\% = 20\% = 0.2$

- Breakeven point (revenue) $= \dfrac{5,400}{0.2} = £27,000$ or $£15 \times 1,800$ units $= £27,000$

- Margin of safety (as a % of budgeted sales) $= \dfrac{3,000 - 1,800}{3,000} \times 100\% = 40\%$

- Sales volume to achieve profit of £3,300 $= \dfrac{£(5,400 + 3,300)}{£3} = 2,900$ units

- The sales volume to achieve a target profit $= \dfrac{\text{Fixed costs + target profit}}{\text{Contribution per unit}}$ (in units)

$$\text{or} = \dfrac{\text{Fixed costs + target profit}}{\text{C/S ratio}} \text{ (in £ revenue)}$$

A limiting factor limits the activities of a business. It could be sales or limited supplies of a resource, such as materials or labour. Management should try to maximise the contribution per unit of the limiting factor.

The optimal production plan

1. Calculate contribution per unit of each product

2. Identify the limiting factor

3. Calculate contribution per unit of limiting factor for each product

4. Rank products

5. Manufacture products in rank order

Assumptions

Contribution is maximised by earning the highest contribution from each unit of limiting factor.

Profit is maximised when contribution is maximised.

Example

1 + **2** Only 10,000 machine hours are available. Product A contributes £2 per unit, and uses 4 machine hours per unit. Product B contributes £1.50 per unit, and uses 1 machine hour per unit. There is demand for 6,000 units of Product A and 6,000 units of Product B.

4 *Rank*

3 Product A: $\dfrac{\text{£2 contribution}}{\text{4 machine hours}}$ = £0.50 per machine hour   2

Product B: $\dfrac{\text{£1.50 contribution}}{\text{1 machine hour}}$ = £1.50 per machine hour   1

£

5 Produce 6,000 Product B: 6,000   machine hours × £1.50   9,000
Produce 1,000 Product A: 4,000   machine hours × £0.50   2,000
                           10,000   Total contribution   11,000

Make or buy decision

- Make internally or contract out
- Comparison of relevant costs
  - Differences in unit variable costs and any directly attributable fixed costs

Closure of a business segment decision

- Close an area of the business either temporarily or permanently
- Will tend to be based upon short-run relevant costs (assuming income from sale of non-current assets covers redundancy costs **or** both items are negligible)

In both cases qualitative factors must also be taken into account

> The basic principle of discounting is that if we wish to have £S in a year's time, we need to invest a certain sum now (year 0) at the interest rate of r% in order to obtain the required sum of money in the future.

Discount factors are shown in present value tables provided in the assessment.

The rate of interest (r%) to be used is often called the **cost of capital**.

Discounting terminology

Time value of money   –   £1 today is worth more than £1 received at a future time because of its investment potential

Net present value   –   The total of the PV of a project's inflows minus the PV of the outflows

Net terminal value   –   The value of an investment at the end of a project's life

Net present cost or life cycle cost   –   The total of the PV of the costs of an operation or decision

10: Decision making techniques

Example: NPV appraisal

Time	Year 0	Year 1	Year 2	Year 3
Outflow = investment	(100,000)	0	0	0
Inflow = revenue **or** cost savings	0	20,000	40,000	80,000
PV factor @ 10%	1.000	0.909	0.826	0.751
Discounted cash flow	(100,000)	18,180	33,040	60,080
Net present value (NPV)	11,300			

This calculation must be based on **cash flow, not profits**.

Notes

Notes

Notes

Notes

Notes